A TRUE BOOK™

DIGGING IN GEOLOGY

# All About Minerals

## Discovering the Building Blocks of Earth

Cody Crane

**Children's Press®**
An Imprint of Scholastic Inc.

**Content Consultants**
Dr. Wen-lu Zhu
Professor of Geology
Department of Geology
University of Maryland, College Park

Library of Congress Cataloging-in-Publication Data
Names: Crane, Cody, author.
Title: All about minerals: discovering the building blocks of Earth / Cody Crane.
Other titles: All about minerals
Description: New York: Children's Press, an imprint of Scholastic Inc., 2021. | Series: Digging in geology |
    Includes index. | Audience: Ages 8-10. | Audience: Grades 4-6. | Summary: "This book introduces readers
    to minerals"—Provided by publisher.
Identifiers: LCCN 2020035263 | ISBN 9780531137116 (library binding) | ISBN 9780531137154 (paperback)
Subjects: LCSH: Mineralogy—Juvenile literature. | Minerals—Juvenile literature.
Classification: LCC QE365.2 .C73 2021 | DDC 549—dc23
LC record available at https://lccn.loc.gov/2020035263

Design by Kathleen Petelinsek
Editorial development by Priyanka Lamichhane

Scholastic Inc., 557 Broadway, New York, NY 10012

1 2 3 4 5 6 7 8 9 10 R 30 29 28 27 26 25 24 23 22 21

**Front cover: Background: a shimmering pile of gold; top: some minerals glow in the dark, including this one called willemite; top right: hot, mineral-rich water sprays out of Fly Geyser, located in Nevada; bottom: colorful mineral deposits surround hot springs in Ethiopia, Africa.**

**Back cover: The Mir diamond mine in Siberia, Russia, is one of the deepest in the world.**

# Find the Truth!

**Everything** you are about to read is true *except* for one of the sentences on this page.

Which one is **TRUE**?

**T or F** People have to dig deep inside Earth to find minerals.

**T or F** Diamonds are the hardest minerals on Earth.

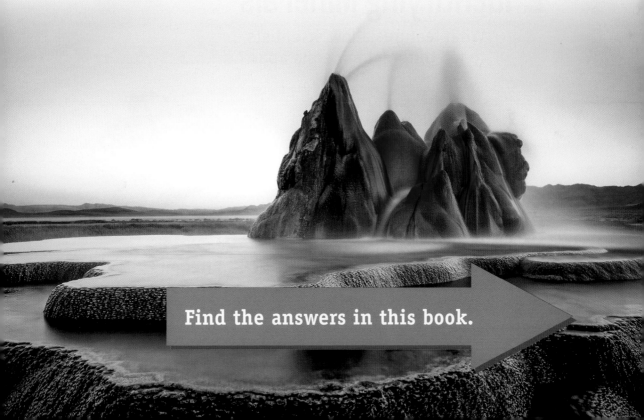

Find the answers in this book.

# What's in This Book?

The **BIG** Truth

## Is It a Rock or a Mineral?

Are these
rocks or
minerals?

4

Minerals are used in some paints.

# 3 Finding Minerals

# 4 The Many Uses of Minerals

Minerals such as gold and copper are used in cell phones.

# Dig In!

**Minerals are substances that form naturally on Earth.** They are made up of one or more **elements,** which are the basic building blocks of everything in the universe. **Minerals are solid crystals.** This means they are made of substances whose atoms are arranged in a repeating, orderly pattern. **Minerals are also inorganic:** they are not made of living things. Some **minerals are gemstones** that can be cut and polished for jewelry.

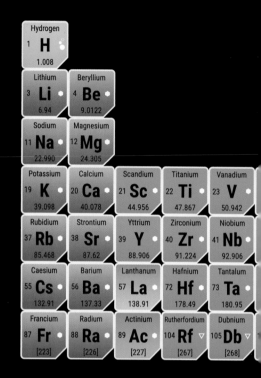

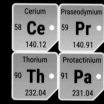

The periodic table is used to organize the 118 known elements. Elements make up minerals.

# PERIODIC TABLE

Beryllium

Element Name

Atomic Number

ment Symbol

**4 Be**

9.0122

State of Matter

Atomic Mass

- Gas
- Liquid
- Solid
- ▽ Unknown

| | | | | | |
|---|---|---|---|---|---|
| | | | | | Helium 2 **He** 4.0026 |
| Boron 5 **B** 10.81 | Carbon 6 **C** 12.011 | Nitrogen 7 **N** 14.007 | Oxygen 8 **O** 15.999 | Fluorine 9 **F** 18.998 | Neon 10 **Ne** 20.180 |
| Aluminium 13 **Al** 26.982 | Silicon 14 **Si** 28.085 | Phosphorus 15 **P** 30.974 | Sulfur 16 **S** 32.06 | Chlorine 17 **Cl** 35.45 | Argon 18 **Ar** 39.88 |

| nium | Manganese 25 **Mn** 54.938 | Iron 26 **Fe** 55.845 | Cobalt 27 **Co** 58.933 | Nickel 28 **Ni** 58.693 | Copper 29 **Cu** 63.546 | Zinc 30 **Zn** 65.38 | Gallium 31 **Ga** 69.723 | Germanium 32 **Ge** 72.630 | Arsenic 33 **As** 74.922 | Selenium 34 **Se** 78.971 | Bromine 35 **Br** 79.904 | Krypton 36 **Kr** 83.798 |
|---|---|---|---|---|---|---|---|---|---|---|---|---|
| **Cr** 996 | | | | | | | | | | | | |

| denum | Technetium 43 **Tc** [97] | Ruthenium 44 **Ru** 101.07 | Rhodium 45 **Rh** 102.91 | Palladium 46 **Pd** 106.42 | Silver 47 **Ag** 107.87 | Cadmium 48 **Cd** 112.41 | Indium 49 **In** 114.82 | Tin 50 **Sn** 118.71 | Antimony 51 **Sb** 121.76 | Tellurium 52 **Te** 127.60 | Iodine 53 **I** 126.90 | Xenon 54 **Xe** 131.29 |
|---|---|---|---|---|---|---|---|---|---|---|---|---|
| **Mo** 95 | | | | | | | | | | | | |

| gsten | Rhenium 75 **Re** 186.21 | Osmium 76 **Os** 190.23 | Iridium 77 **Ir** 192.22 | Platinum 78 **Pt** 195.08 | Gold 79 **Au** 196.97 | Mercury 80 **Hg** 200.59 | Thallium 81 **Tl** 204.38 | Lead 82 **Pb** 207.2 | Bismuth 83 **Bi** 208.98 | Polonium 84 **Po** [209] | Astatine 85 **At** [210] | Radon 86 **Rn** [222] |
|---|---|---|---|---|---|---|---|---|---|---|---|---|
| **W** 8.84 | | | | | | | | | | | | |

| orgium | Bohrium 107 **Bh** [270] | Hassium 108 **Hs** [269] | Meitnerium 109 **Mt** [278] | Darmstadtium 110 **Ds** [281] | Roentgenium 111 **Rg** [282] | Copernicium 112 **Cn** [285] | Nihonium 113 **Nh** [286] | Flerovium 114 **Fl** [289] | Moscovium 115 **Mc** [290] | Livermorium 116 **Lv** [293] | Tennessine 117 **Ts** [294] | Oganesson 118 **Og** [294] |
|---|---|---|---|---|---|---|---|---|---|---|---|---|
| **Sg** 69] | | | | | | | | | | | | |

| ymium | Promethium 61 **Pm** [145] | Samarium 62 **Sm** 150.36 | Europium 63 **Eu** 151.96 | Gadolinium 64 **Gd** 157.25 | Terbium 65 **Tb** 158.93 | Dysprosium 66 **Dy** 162.50 | Holmium 67 **Ho** 164.93 | Erbium 68 **Er** 167.26 | Thulium 69 **Tm** 168.93 | Ytterbium 70 **Yb** 173.05 | Lutetium 71 **Lu** 174.97 |
|---|---|---|---|---|---|---|---|---|---|---|---|
| **Nd** 4.24 | | | | | | | | | | | |

| U | Neptunium 93 **Np** [237] | Plutonium 94 **Pu** [244] | Americium 95 **Am** [243] | Curium 96 **Cm** [247] | Berkelium 97 **Bk** [247] | Californium 98 **Cf** [251] | Einsteinium 99 **Es** [252] | Fermium 100 **Fm** [257] | Mendelevium 101 **Md** [258] | Nobelium 102 **No** [259] | Lawrencium 103 **Lr** [266] |
|---|---|---|---|---|---|---|---|---|---|---|---|
| 8.03 | | | | | | | | | | | |

**Minerals are also building blocks for rocks.** They make up rocks that, in turn, make up our planet.

Minerals at these hot springs create odd formations.

Brightly colored mineral deposits surround hot springs in Dallol, Ethiopia, in Africa.

CHAPTER

# How Minerals Form

There are more than 5,000 types of minerals. Some minerals such as diamonds contain just one type of element: diamonds are made of only the element carbon. Other minerals are made up of a mixture of elements. Calcite, the main mineral in chalk, is a mixture of the elements carbon, calcium, and oxygen. Elements combine to form minerals through processes inside Earth and on its surface. Read on to find out how this happens.

Stalactites and stalagmites grow less than 0.04 inch (1 millimeter) a year.

The world's largest salt flat, Salar de Uyuni, in Bolivia, was once an ancient lake.

# Left Behind

Long ago, some areas of our planet contained shallow lakes or seas. Heat from the sun caused their water to **evaporate**. Eventually, the water completely disappeared. Minerals such as salt that **dissolved**, or mixed, into the water were left behind. Similar processes happen in some caves. Carbon dioxide escapes from the water when it drips into caves. Minerals **precipitate**, or come out of the liquid, out of the less acidic water and create icicle-like formations called stalactites and stalagmites.

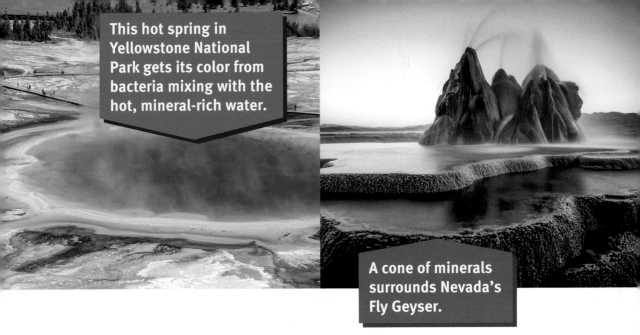

This hot spring in Yellowstone National Park gets its color from bacteria mixing with the hot, mineral-rich water.

A cone of minerals surrounds Nevada's Fly Geyser.

## In Hot Water

Inside Earth, melted rock called **magma** rises toward the surface. The magma heats water underground, causing minerals to dissolve in the liquid. The mineral-rich water can trickle into cracks in surrounding rocks. As the water cools, solid minerals precipitate and fill the cracks. If the water reaches the surface, it can form a hot spring or erupt as a geyser. Minerals also precipitate from the water as it cools around these landforms, creating unique formations.

# Cool Down

Magma itself can cool and harden into minerals. Temperature affects how mineral crystals form. Slower-cooling magma creates larger crystals. Faster-cooling magma creates smaller crystals. Sometimes magma cools too quickly for crystals to form. The result is a smooth, black material known as obsidian, or volcanic glass. Even though it forms naturally, is a solid, and is inorganic, obsidian is not a mineral because it does not have a crystal structure.

Magma that reaches Earth's surface is called lava. Here, lava flows out of an erupting volcano.

obsidian, or volcanic glass

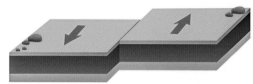

**Movement of Tectonic Plates**

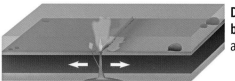

**Divergent plate boundary:** Plates moving away from each other

**Transform plate boundary:** Plates sliding past each other

**Convergent plate boundary:** Plates pushing against and slipping under each other

# Under Pressure

Earth's uppermost layer is made of **tectonic plates**, giant, slow-moving rock slabs. The boundary of two tectonic plates can be categorized into three types: divergent plate boundaries where plates move away from each other, transform plate boundaries where plates slide past each other, and convergent plate boundaries where plates push against each other and one slides beneath the other. These movements can expose rocks to extreme heat and pressure. This changes their minerals and transforms them into **metamorphic rocks**.

## Below the Surface

Most types of minerals are found in Earth's crust, or surface layer. But minerals also exist much deeper inside Earth's mantle. The mantle is the planet's second and largest layer. Most diamonds formed in the mantle. This happened long ago, during the first few billion years of the planet's history. Magma then carried rocks containing diamonds and other minerals to the surface.

# Minerals Found in Earth's Layers

Earth is made up of four distinct layers. Peek inside our planet to discover where minerals are found.

## Crust

**Depth: 0–22 miles (0–35 kilometers)**
Earth's rocky outer layer forms the land and seafloor; the largest variety of minerals are found here. The most common are feldspar, quartz, pyroxenes, and amphiboles.

## Mantle

**Depth: 22–1,800 miles (35–2,900 km)**
Earth's second layer is made of solid rock. Minerals found in the mantle include olivine, pyroxenes, and bridgmanite.

## Outer Core

**Depth: 1,800–3,200 miles (2,900–5,100 km)**
This layer surrounding Earth's inner core is made up of the melted metal elements iron and nickel.

## Inner Core

**Depth: 3,200–4,000 miles (5,100–6,400 km)**
Earth's center is made up of solid iron and nickel.

Some minerals have the ability to glow when exposed to **ultraviolet light**.

Some varieties of the mineral calcite can glow red, white, blue, green, pink, and even orange.

# Identifying Minerals

All minerals have unique features based on their chemical makeup. Scientists called **mineralogists** use these characteristics to tell minerals apart. Common properties mineralogists look for when studying a mineral are its color, luster, hardness, and streak. Let's find out how these features help them tell minerals apart.

# Color

Minerals come in many colors! But color alone may not be enough for a mineralogist to identify a mineral. This is because minerals can contain impurities or other defects that affect their color. Pure quartz, for example, is clear. But other forms of this mineral contain impurities, creating quartz in almost every color. Also, some minerals can look alike. The mineral pyrite is nicknamed "fool's gold" because it looks so much like gold.

Rubies are known for their bold red color.

Aurichalcite (nonmetallic, pearly luster)

Quartz (nonmetallic, glassy luster)

From shiny to glassy to dull, minerals have a variety of different lusters.

Barite (nonmetallic, shiny to pearly luster)

Feldspar (nonmetallic, glassy luster)

Bornite (metallic, shiny luster)

Some minerals appear to change color depending on how light reflects off of them.

# Luster

Luster refers to how a mineral glitters, shimmers, or shines. It describes the way light reflects, or bounces, off of it. There are two main kinds of luster: metallic and nonmetallic. A metallic luster describes minerals with a mirror-like shine. Nonmetallic lusters can be slick like the surface of glass or pearly like the inside of a shell, sparkly like a diamond, and even dull like the chalky mineral kaolinite.

# Hardness

Mineralogists rely on the Mohs' Hardness Scale to determine how soft or hard a mineral is. This includes minerals and common objects of a known hardness. Mineralogists scrape the materials listed on the scale against the surface of an unknown mineral. A scratch means the mineral is softer than the material. No scratch means the mineral is harder. Minerals usually have a specific hardness, so identifying where an unknown mineral falls on the scale can help reveal its identity.

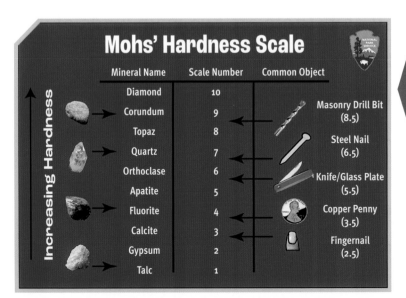

## Mohs' Hardness Scale

| Mineral Name | Scale Number | Common Object |
|---|---|---|
| Diamond | 10 | |
| Corundum | 9 | Masonry Drill Bit (8.5) |
| Topaz | 8 | |
| Quartz | 7 | Steel Nail (6.5) |
| Orthoclase | 6 | Knife/Glass Plate (5.5) |
| Apatite | 5 | |
| Fluorite | 4 | Copper Penny (3.5) |
| Calcite | 3 | |
| Gypsum | 2 | Fingernail (2.5) |
| Talc | 1 | |

Increasing Hardness

German mineralogist Friedrich Mohs created his hardness scale in 1812.

Hematite produces a rust-colored streak because it contains iron.

Hematite and magnetite look similar. Mineralogists can tell them apart because magnetite's streak is black and hematite's is reddish brown.

## Streak

Streak is the color of the powdered form of a mineral. A streak test can help identify a mineral. This is how it works: A mineralogist scrapes the sample across a ceramic tile. A streak of crumbled mineral, sometimes a different color than the whole mineral, is left behind. While a specific mineral's color can vary, its streak is always the same, helping narrow down its identity. A streak test can also help tell two similar-looking minerals apart.

# Tools of the Trade

Here are some tools mineralogists use to take samples of minerals in the field and identify them. They sometimes identify new substances that can have new uses in different industries. Mineralogists can also help mining companies locate and dig up minerals from Earth. Thanks to the work mineralogists do, we can learn more about what Earth is made of!

1. **Rock hammer:** used to chip off samples of minerals
2. **Geological compass:** helps determine location, orientation, and slope of rock layers
3. **Shaded relief map:** shows the shape of the land features on Earth's surface
4. **Mohs' hardness testing kit or penknife:** used to scratch minerals to determine their hardness
5. **Streak plate:** used to perform streak tests in the field
6. **Pocket magnifier:** a foldable lens to look closely at minerals

# Classifying Minerals

Minerals in each group share a similar chemical makeup. This allows mineralogists to classify, or organize, related minerals into the following groups.

| Mineral Groups | Mineral Features | Mineral Example |
|---|---|---|
| Native elements | These minerals are made of only one element and fall into three categories:<br>• metals: hard, shiny materials that can be shaped and allow heat and electricity to flow through them<br>• semimetals: materials with properties of both metals and nonmetals<br>• nonmetals: materials that don't allow heat or electricity to flow through them, are not shiny, and can't be shaped | Gold |
| Sulfides | Sulfides contain the element sulfur combined with a metal or a semimetal. | Galena |
| Sulfates | Sulfates are made of sulfur combined with metals and the element oxygen. | Barite |
| Oxides | Oxides are made of a metal combined with the element oxygen. | Hematite |
| Silicates | Silicates are the largest known group of minerals. They contain metals combined with the elements silicon and oxygen. | Mica |
| Halides | Halides form when a metal combines with the elements bromine, chlorine, fluorine, or iodine. | Halite |
| Carbonates | Carbonates contain the elements oxygen and carbon, plus one or more metals. | Malachite |

# Is It a Rock or a Mineral?

Minerals are basic building blocks of rocks. Rocks and minerals are similar, but they are not the same! Check out the diagram below to find out the similarities and differences between them.

## Rocks versus Minerals

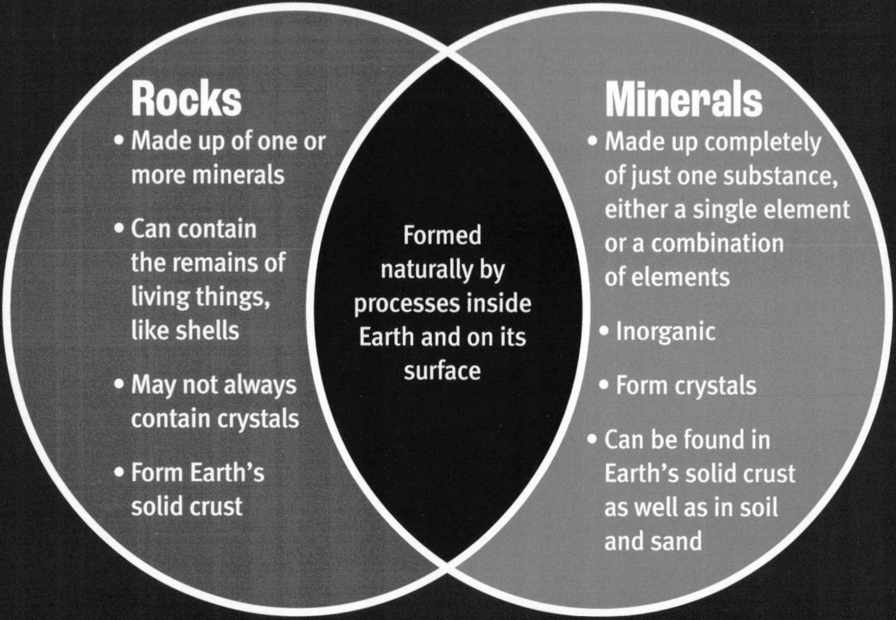

### Rocks

- Made up of one or more minerals

- Can contain the remains of living things, like shells

- May not always contain crystals

- Form Earth's solid crust

**Formed naturally by processes inside Earth and on its surface**

### Minerals

- Made up completely of just one substance, either a single element or a combination of elements

- Inorganic

- Form crystals

- Can be found in Earth's solid crust as well as in soil and sand

# The Building Blocks of Granite

Granite is a rock that makes up much of Earth's rocky outer layer, the layer of rocks that form the land. Check out how four minerals come together to create granite!

**Quartz:** The second most common mineral in granite. It appears as round, glassy grains. Quartz, along with feldspar, makes granite extremely hard.

**Feldspar:** The most abundant mineral in granite. It appears as white or pink crystals.

GRANITE

**Mica:** This mineral has a pearly luster. Tiny grains of mica make granite sparkle.

**Hornblende:** The mineral that gives granite dark-colored spots.

*Mineral* comes from the Latin word *mineralis*, which means "something mined."

The Mir diamond mine in Siberia, Russia, is so deep the Empire State Building could fit inside and still not reach the top.

# Finding Minerals

A mineral's worth depends on how difficult it is to dig up in large amounts. But before companies can extract minerals, mineralogists have to find them. First they look at an area's land features, which provide hints about what minerals lie below the surface. Then they test the area's rocks and soil. This helps locate spots likely to have **ores,** rocks that contain useful minerals.

This machine is more than 30 stories tall.

This excavator used to strip-mine in Germany is the world's largest land vehicle.

# Big Dig

Some minerals are found closer to the surface than others. This is because minerals can be pushed up from deep underground as Earth's tectonic plates slowly shift and move. Workers can access these minerals by removing strips of land. This process is known as strip-mining. If mineral deposits at the surface extend farther down, companies may opt to dig a giant pit. These mines grow deeper and deeper until all the minerals are found and extracted.

# Going Underground

Minerals located deep within Earth's crust are mined by digging underground tunnels. Ore is drilled, blasted, or cut away from the surrounding rock. Then it is carried by trucks and conveyors or lifted in containers up to the surface. Underground mining is dangerous. Miners inhale lots of dust, which can harm their health. Fresh air is pumped into the mine so they can breathe. Miners face the threat of tunnels collapsing. The salt in Cargill mine is left over from a sea that existed 400 million years ago.

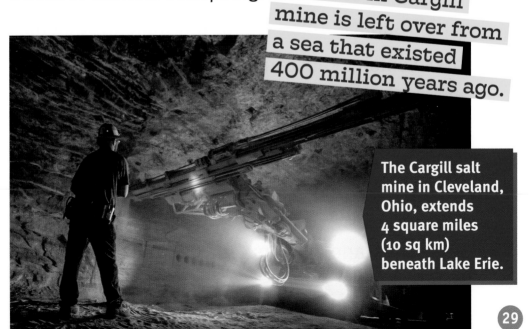

The Cargill salt mine in Cleveland, Ohio, extends 4 square miles (10 sq km) beneath Lake Erie.

Visitors to Crater of Diamonds State Park have found more than 33,100 diamonds since the park opened in 1972.

People can pan, or sift, through gravel in riverbeds to find minerals.

## Exposed!

People do not always need to dig to find minerals. Wind or water can **erode**, or wear away, rocks at Earth's surface. This exposes any minerals that the rocks contain. Rain can then wash the exposed minerals into streams, where they gather. Earthquakes and erupting volcanoes can also push rocks to the surface. This happened at Crater of Diamonds State Park in Arkansas. It is the site of an ancient volcano. Visitors can find precious minerals on the ground, and they get to keep them!

# Environmental Impact

Mining provides people with important natural resources.
But it can have a big impact on the environment.

### Damaging Nature

Mining near the surface destroys wilderness and animal homes. This land in Indonesia is being prepared for copper mining. You can see the bare land where trees have been cut down.

### Producing Pollution

Chemicals, like acids, can release toxic metals into the environment. These substances can pollute soil and waterways. In 2015, mine waste polluted the Animas River in Colorado (seen here), changing the color of the water.

### Lost Landscape

Without trees and plants, water and wind can erode the land. Removing rock and soil while mining underground can weaken the ground above, causing it to cave in. Work in a nearby underground mine caused this large hole in Mexico in 2018.

Every person in the United States uses about 19 tons (17 metric tons) of minerals each year.

Minerals are found everywhere, in light bulbs, cell phones, and even makeup.

# The Many Uses of Minerals

You might not realize it, but you encounter minerals every day. You can find them in your classroom, in your home, even in your car. Minerals on their own are needed to make things such as bricks and laundry detergent. Minerals are also the source of important elements, such as metals. Take a look at the many ways we use minerals.

# Minerals at Home

Lots of things in your home contain minerals. Even many parts of your home itself were made using minerals.

**Makeup:** talc used as a base for face powder

**Shingles:** feldspar, quartz

**Car:** iron from the minerals hematite and magnetite

**Laundry detergent:** borax, a type of cleaner, made from the mineral kernite

This diagram shows some of the minerals you may find where you live.

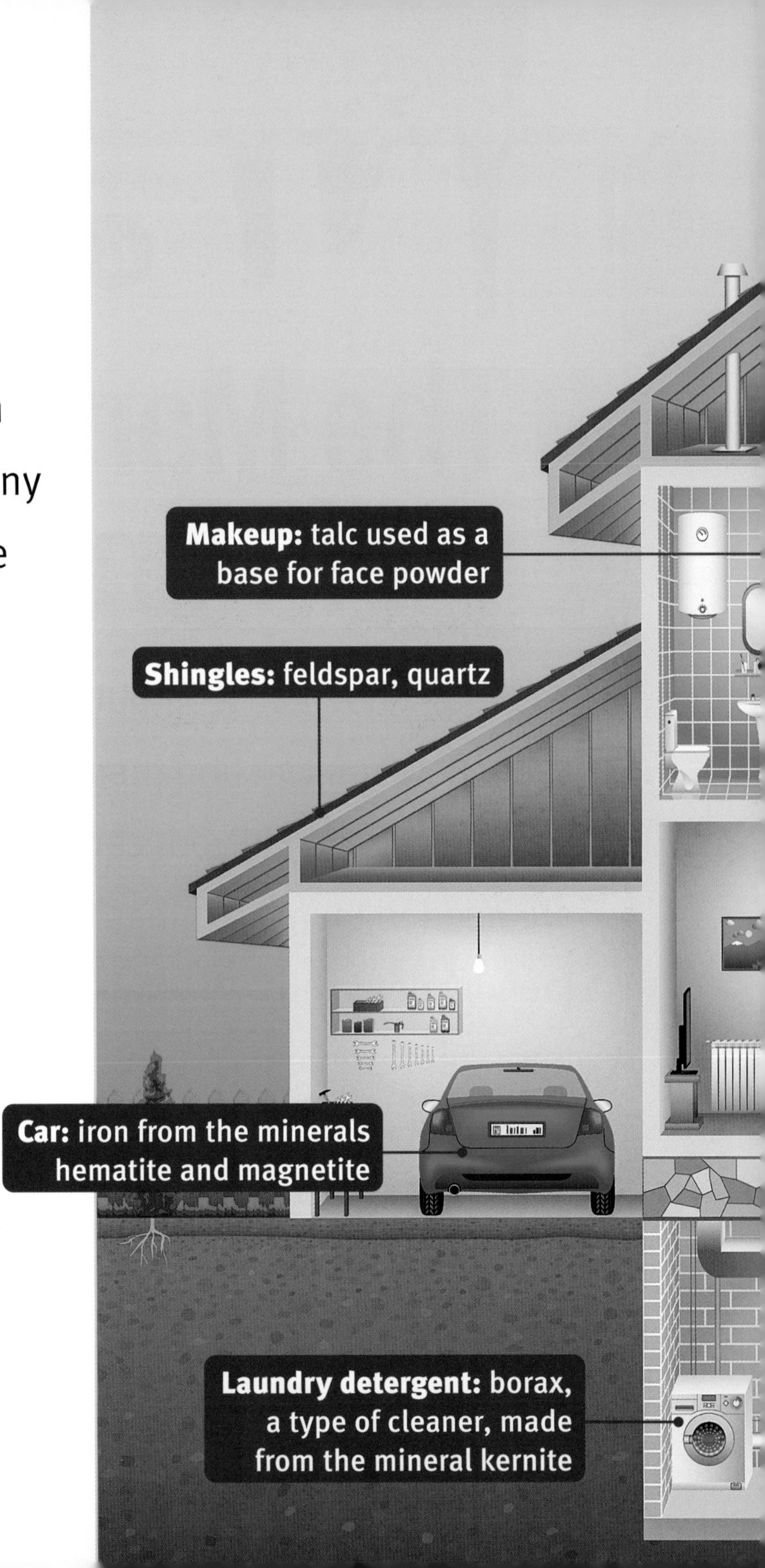

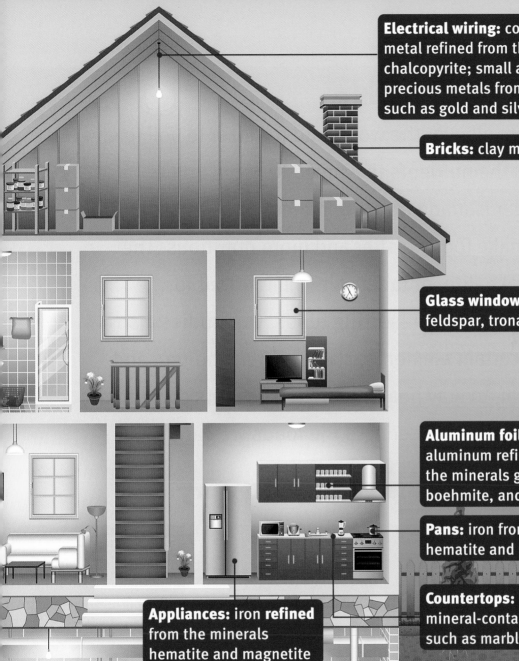

**Electrical wiring:** copper metal refined from the mineral chalcopyrite; small amounts of precious metals from minerals such as gold and silver

**Bricks:** clay minerals

**Glass windows:** calcite, feldspar, trona, quartz

**Aluminum foil and cans:** aluminum refined from the minerals gibbsite, boehmite, and diaspore

**Pans:** iron from the minerals hematite and magnetite

**Countertops:** made from mineral-containing rocks, such as marble and granite

**Appliances:** iron **refined** from the minerals hematite and magnetite

**Cement:** a mix of calcite, clay, gypsum

# Feeding the World

Farmers all over the world add fertilizer to soil to give plants the nutrients they need to grow. Some fertilizer is made from the mineral sylvite. Minerals also make foods tastier and more nutritious. The mineral halite, or table salt, is important for seasoning and preserving foods. Our bodies also need certain elements, such as iron, sodium, and calcium, to stay healthy. Those elements come from minerals introduced into the foods we eat.

## Timeline: Minerals Through History

**10 THOUSAND YEARS AGO**
During the Stone Age people use the mineral jade to make tools, clay for bricks, and gemstones to carve beads.

**5,100–2,300 YEARS AGO**
Ancient Egyptians use gold and gemstones to decorate pharaohs' burial chambers.

**2,140 YEARS AGO**
The oldest known pills, made by Romans, contain zinc minerals to treat sore eyes.

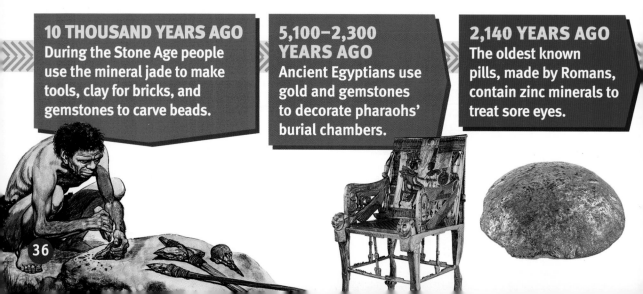

# High-Tech Minerals

It is likely you watched TV or chatted on a cell phone recently. All electronic devices have parts made of metals from ores. Some run on rechargeable batteries that contain the element lithium, which comes from minerals. The tiny computer chips that control electronics are made from silica from the mineral quartz. People have been finding uses for minerals for thousands of years. Today, we rely on these materials to make our modern lives possible. What new uses for minerals will we think of in the future?

**850 CE**
In China, a mineral called niter is used to make gunpowder, creating the first fireworks and, later, weapons.

**1546**
German scientist Georgius Agricola writes the first textbook categorizing minerals.

**1927**
A Canadian scientist builds the first clock containing the mineral quartz, which allows it to keep very accurate time.

**1958**
The International Mineralogical Association is founded. It approves names for newly discovered minerals.

# 10 Magnificent Mineral Facts!

**1** Gems such as diamonds are rare minerals that have been cut and polished and are prized for their beauty.

**2** All birthstones are minerals.

**3** Ice is considered a mineral because it is a natural substance, has a crystal structure, and is inorganic.

**6** Although sugar has a crystal structure, it is not a mineral because it is made up of organic material.

**7** Nearly half of all minerals are named after people. The mineral armalcolite was named after astronauts Neil Armstrong (pictured), Buzz Aldrin, and Michael Collins.

**5** The most abundant mineral on Earth is bridgmanite, found only in Earth's mantle.

**4** Meteorites, space rocks that land on Earth, are mainly made up of five minerals.

**9** Most mineral names end in the suffix "ite"—for example, calcite.

**8** Lodestones, naturally occurring magnets, are made of the mineral magnetite (pictured).

**10** Iron ore minerals, such as magnetite and hematite, are the most mined minerals.

# Name That Mineral

**Mineralogists identify minerals based on a variety of physical properties.** Four of those features are color, luster, hardness, and streak. The table on page 41 shows these characteristics for different minerals. Study the table, and then answer the questions below.

## Analyze It!

1. Which two minerals have the same hardness?

2. Calcite and kaolinite have the same crystal and streak color. What other features could help tell them apart?

3. A mineralogist has a sample with a green color and a glassy luster. What minerals might it be?

4. Why might mineralogists need to use multiple features to tell apart a sample of halite and feldspar? Explain your reasoning.

# Mineral Physical Property Chart

| Mineral | Color | Luster | Hardness | Streak |
|---------|-------|--------|----------|--------|
| Calcite | white | glassy | 3 | white |
| Halite | white, colorless | glassy | 2 | white |
| Flourite | green, purple | glassy | 4 | white |
| Feldspar | white, brown, gray, pink | glassy | 6–6.5 | white |
| Kaolinite | white | dull | 1.5–2 | white |
| Olivine | green | glassy | 6.5–7 | hard to crumble and leave a streak |
| Pyrite | yellow | metallic | 6–6.5 | greenish black |
| Talc | white, green, gray | pearly | 1 | white |

# Grow a Stalactite

Stalactites take thousands of years to form as water slowly drips into caves. Here is a faster way to grow one of these rocking mineral formations.

## Materials

Two glass jars
Warm water
Food coloring
Spoon
Epsom salt
Saucer
Scissors
String
Two paper clips

## Directions

**1** Fill the two jars to the top with warm tap water. Add a few drops of food coloring to each jar.

**2** Stir one spoonful of Epsom salt at a time into both jars until no more will dissolve.

**3** Set the saucer between the two jars.

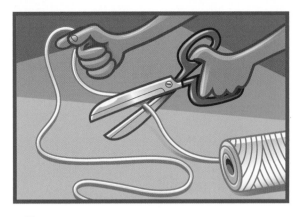

**4** Cut a piece of string long enough to stretch between the two jars and hang halfway into each.

**5** Tie a paper clip as a weight to each end of the string. Put the end of each string into a jar.

**6** Leave the jars for a few weeks until a stalactite forms on the string. You can add more Epsom salt and water to the jars to keep it growing.

# Explain It!

Using what you learned in the book, can you explain what happened in this activity? If you need help, turn back to page 10.

# True Statistics

The width of Utah's Bingham Canyon Mine, a source of copper ore and the world's largest open-pit mine: 2.5 miles (4 km)

The amount of mineral halite (table salt) that would form if all of the ocean water on Earth evaporated: 39,000,000,000,000,000 tons—enough to spread it evenly over Earth's surface in a layer 500 feet (152 m) thick

The weight of the Cullinan Diamond, thought to be the largest ever discovered: 1.37 pounds (0.6 kg)

The amount Nevada, the top mineral-producing state in the United States, makes each year from mining minerals: $7.8 billion

The length of the world's longest stalactite, found in Jeita Grotto in Lebanon: 27 feet (8.2 m)

How far below Earth's surface the world's deepest mines extend: 2 miles (3 km)

## Did you find the truth?

**F** People have to dig deep inside Earth to find minerals.

**T** Diamonds are the hardest minerals on Earth.

# Resources

## Other books in this series:

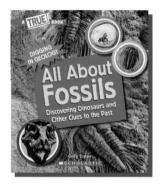

## You can also look at:

Brown, Cynthia Light. *Rocks and Minerals! With 25 Science Projects for Kids*. Vermont: Nomad Press, 2020.

Farndon, John. *Rocks, Minerals and Gems*. Richmond Hill, Canada: Firefly Books, 2016.

Love, Ann and Jane Drake. *America at Work: Mining*. Toronto, Canada: Kids Can Press, 2002.

# Glossary

**crystals** (KRIS-tuhls): solids whose atoms are arranged in a repeating pattern

**dissolved** (di-ZAHLVD): when a substance breaks down when mixed into a liquid

**elements** (EL-uh-muhnts): substances made of a single type of atom; the basic building blocks of matter

**erode** (i-RODE): to wear away

**evaporate** (i-VAP-uh-rate): to change from a liquid to a gas

**magma** (MAG-muh): melted rock beneath Earth's surface

**metamorphic rocks** (met-uh-MOR-fik rahks): rocks changed by heat, pressure, or chemical reactions into another type of rock

**mineralogists** (mih-ner-AH-loh-jists): scientists who study minerals

**ores** (ors): rocks that contain valuable minerals

**precipitate** (pri-SIP-i-tate): to separate a solid from a liquid it is dissolved in

**refined** (ree-FINED): having had unwanted materials removed

**tectonic plates** (tech-TAH-nik playts): giant slow-moving rock slabs that make up Earth's crust and the uppermost portion of the mantle

**ultraviolet light** (uhl-truh-VYE-lit lite): a type of light that cannot be seen by the human eye. It is given off by the sun.

# Index

Page numbers in **bold** indicate illustrations.

# About the Author

Cody Crane is an award-winning children's writer, specializing in nonfiction. She studied science and environmental reporting at New York University. Before becoming an author, she was set on being a scientist. She later discovered that writing about science could be just as fun as doing the real thing. She lives in Houston, Texas, with her husband and son.